The Strange Voice

The wonder sight

By

Bernard Benson Sarfo

The Strange Voice

Bernard Benson Sarfo

Published by Bernard Benson Sarfo, 2024.

THE STRANGE VOICE

First edition. April 21, 2024.

ISBN: 979-8224949915

Written by Bernard Benson Sarfo.

Also by Bernard Benson Sarfo

The Fact Among Facts (1st)
The Fact Among Facts

Standalone
The Youth Murderer
Be Original Not a Copy
The Christians Science or Scholarship
Precious than Paradise
Habit makes future
A shelter from storm and rain
The Science of Life
The Strongest Lion Knockback
The Perfect and Inspiring City
Above Hope, Faith and Love
The Hero's Brave Decisions
The Weakest Among Plants
The Hero's Brave Decisions
Doing Above The Ability
The Wisdom Beyond Power And Greatness

Heavier Than the Heavens
The Academics Brains and Recreation Logics
The Strange Voice

Dedication

I dedicate this book to everyone in the world today.

'When wisdom entered into your heart, and knowledge is pleasant unto your soul, discretion shall preserve you, understanding shall keep you' (Proverbs 2:10, 11).

Introduction

What makes you wonder? What are you looking? What impress you? One day Moses went to the wilderness of Midian with his father-in-law flock. He came to the mountain of God.

The Angel appeared to him in the flames of fire in the bush. The bush was on the fire but it did not burn up. It was a wonder sight, so he went and see why the bush does not burn up. God called him from within the burning bush Moses! Moses!

He responded here I am. Do not come closer, God said but take off your sandals, for the place where you are standing is holy ground. It is a wonder sight and terrible. It was a first experience, and no one has seen such a wonderful sight before.

In fact, Moses was shocked to see such a sight, and he wondered. God intend to rescue the Israelites through Moses. Their cry reached the ear of the Lord of host and He was concerned about their suffering. Moses was afraid to go to Egypt and rescue the Israelites.

As Christians, God is sending us to go and rescue those are in the world. We should not fear to go and rescue our brothers who the world has bought their mind.

He is I am that I am, all power belongs to Him. He is sending us to go into the entire world to preach the Gospel and make disciples for Him.

Is there anyone who can tell where God comes from or describe the beginning of God? Is God begot by someone or has He had the one who created Him?

Is there any answer for it or can somebody answer me? We human beings have no answer and Heaven Angels do not know.

He is God! He came by Himself and has no Mother or Father and has no Creator. He is I am that I am and there is none to compare or be the same as Him.

He is God! Many people have failed and others have had madness concerning where God come from? Hello, world! I want you to know more about God and to fear Him.

We cannot describe God and cannot compare any image with Him. But we are His image and likeness. What does that mean?

Means God created us to act and move like Him but not being in the same body. We are inferior and like nothing before Him.

We are only His creatures; likeness and image for us to be in the form that we can talk with Him as managers of His creation. In all, we need to worship and praise Him for such a chance or opportunity given to us as human beings.

We are to fear God and give glory to Him every day and night. We were nowhere and do not know how we became human beings.

We cannot tell and do not have any idea why we existed as human beings? I want you to know who God is and the reasons why we must fear and tremble before Him.

This book is giving us the knowledge of God and His love towards us. The heavens and the earth will tell you more of God and nature will let you know who God is. He is I am that I am and there is none to compare and be the same. He is the ALPHA and OMEGA.

Contents

1. Do not draw near 2. This is my name forever 3. I am not eloquent

1. Do not draw near

When Moses thought to go and see the wonder sight, God called him not to come closer. For where he was standing was holy ground. We need to be careful and behavior well in sight of God.

In the presences of God our act and doings must be a decent. Our appearance must well presentable and unique. Moses was told not to come closer and he was command to take off his sandals, for the place where he stands is holy ground.

Moses hid his face for he was afraid to look at God. Today, are we afraid to act and dress well in the presence of God? What are we doing in the house of the Lord today? Our Lord is a consuming fire, He is just and righteous.

He loves and want us good. He is near to rescue and comforts us. Our nature as human beings cannot stand before God.

We are sinful beings and unworthy to stand before Him. But He is merciful and gracious and do not want us to be lost but that we should come to repentance. In fact, our nature cannot be able to stand before God, even when He allows us to come before Him.

One thing we need to know is that God do not want us to perish in our sins, but to have an everlasting life. Moses was favored and honored by God. He became the leader of the people of God in the time he has no idea.

What will be your lot and who knows the ends of his or her journey in this life? We must be careful and live wisely, for we do not know when God will approach us. Maybe one will say I am not worthy to be selected by God.

But maybe you are the most sinful man like me or Paul, but God wants to send you to Egypt to deliver His people who are in bondage of sin. God always save sinners and lead sinners to rescue sinners.

This means that, God will not send Heaven Angels to spread His message to the world but He will use you and me who are sinners to go for sinners.

He has prepared His banquet and wants us to eat together with Him. In fact, we are not worthy to come closer to God, but He wants us to be with Him.

This is the love God that whiles we were yet sinners Christ die for us and we are accepted to be called the sons of God.

We need to respect God deeply and fear before Him. We have been welcome by God as Moses, what we need to do is to go as He has sent us.

Many people are suffering and they have no one to help them. It is our duty to help and rescue them from sin bondage.

Oh! Who will go as the Master has commanded? People are dying with no hope and others are suffering severely in their life matters.

Let's consider and do our part as we can for the Master. As Moses was favored in the presence of God, so we are favored today to go and rescue His people from Egypt. That is, those who have lost hope in their life in today's world.

2. This is my name forever

Let's think of God and how He loved us. We are His image and likeness. He has put His name upon us; we are His children from now to the end of age. God identify Himself to Moses in the wilderness of Midian through the burning bush.

Moses has never heard the voice of God before and was afraid when he first heard Him. God told him to go to Egypt and rescue

His people; the Israelites. Moses was afraid to go to Egypt for he thought Pharaoh was seeking to kill him.

God told him that those who were seeking to kill you are dead. But Moses still doubted and afraid that Israel will not believe him about his message. He hesitated and did not want to go with such a message difficult to believe by his brothers.

He questioned God about His name and wanted something that will make his journey meaningful and trusted. Here, he hasn't experienced God before and never known His activities. He wanted to know who God is and what He (God) can do differently from men act and doings. God gave him a sign and prove His divinity and power concerning his journey.

In order for Moses to remember Him, God mentioned Abraham; Isaac and Jacob his fathers to let him know who is sending him (Moses). Our history determines our fame and background and shows the kind of people we are.

God reminded Moses about his history and the one who is talking to him. He made mentioned His name to him. In fact, our life on this earth needs history and the name that will have recognition.

If not, our mission on this earth will have partial recognition but not total. Abraham made a beautiful life and leave best records for his future generation. We need to make a worthy life and the best records for our future generation.

In fact, many people have fail of meaningful life and the life worthy to be praise and recognize. God identify Himself to Moses and remind him of his fathers by putting His name on them for recognition.

Can you imagine why God has putting His name on Abraham; Isaac and Jacob? This shows the love of God towards man and His willing to make us fame. It is a great thing that God will mention His with your name!

Have you thought of this before or what name do you want at the end of age? The name that God gave to Moses was I am that I am, and He further said; I am has sent me to you.

He said to Moses; say to the Israelites, The Lord, the God of your fathers the God of Abraham, the God of Isaac and the God of Jacob has sent me to you.

This is my name forever, the name you shall call me from generation to generation. Do you want God name on you?

3. I am not eloquent

We all have something that makes us well being. It is a mistake to say I am not eloquent as told by Moses before God.

As Christians, Our life is not ours to plan for best and future hope but our duty is to live as His word commanded us.

Moses was afraid to go to Egypt due to fear and lack of knowledge. He (God) knows the thoughts and plans He has for us. It is a thought of peace but of not evil to give us future and great expectation.

Fear of fail has shouted many people's knowledge which can deliver others from bondage of poverty. For the lack of knowledge many people perish and destroy by poverty. We are the creatures of God and image and likeness as well.

We can do everything by His grace and guide. We should not fear failing or discourage by any circumstance that comes in our way. It is our helping tools that make us wellbeing.

God has sent us in whatever field we are and want us to do our best as we can. People are dying and others have lost hope of happiness life.

Many people have been charm not to prosper in life. Others have been prisoned by poverty. What are you doing? What is your duty? Never say you cannot do something for the Master.

Never be a lazy in your labor but do your best and then relief others by your gift. You need to go Egypt and rescue the people who have been imprisoned by the Egyptians.

Means we must go to the world and preach the Gospel to them and then deliver them from sin bondage.

You have what makes you and you can do above what you think; if you allow God to lead you. Paul said I can do all things through

Christ who strengthen me and said, I live by the grace of God. Means we can do everything by the grace and strength of God.

You are eloquent and you can do all things by the grace of God. You should not fear but go as you have been sent by God. He is with us and will teach us what to say and do. Let's read from the Bible;

Exodus 4:10-12

[10]Moses said to the Lord, "Pardon your servant, Lord. I have never been eloquent, neither in the past nor since you have spoken to your servant. I am slow of speech and tongue."

[11]The Lord said to him, "Who gave human beings their mouths? Who makes them deaf or mute? Who gives them sight or makes them blind? Is it not I, the Lord? [12]Now go; I will help you speak and will teach you what to say."

We must be ready for the Master and go as He has commanded us. He is with us until the end of age. Never say I cannot but say here I am. We can do what cannot be margined and can rescue people through our little knowledge we have, and then make them better by helping them with our gift.

Note this text; Exodus 4:19- 23

Now the Lord had said to Moses in Midian, "Go back to Egypt, for all those who wanted to kill you are dead." [20]So Moses took his wife and sons, put them on a donkey and started back to Egypt. And he took the staff of God in his hand.

[21]The Lord said to Moses, "When you return to Egypt, see that you perform before Pharaoh all the wonders I have given you the power to do. But I will harden his heart so that he will not let the people go. [22]Then say to Pharaoh,

'This is what the Lord says: Israel is my firstborn son, [23]and I told you, "Let my son go, so he may worship me." But you refused to let him go; so I will kill your firstborn son.'"

We must use all our gift and knowledge to rescue people from bondage of sin and poverty. Moses was told by God to perform all the miracles before Pharaoh; so we must do as did God commanded Moses. Consider yourself and what you can do for the Master. Never say I am not eloquent.

4. This is Life Eternal

The world has a history about the beginning and the end of creation. The world has the Owner or the Creator who need recognition of every moment. Our history as human beings has a lot to say. We are here for a purpose and the reasons which need everyday attention.

Many people do not understand life and what it is about. Others do not mind what is coming into the world at the end of this age.

What will be the end history of this world? What must we know and cherish? What will be the destiny of this world? Or what will happen at the end of the world?

What must we do and what must we know? This is eternal life that we must know the Father (God) and the Son (Jesus Christ) whom He sent.

How must we know God and the Christ Whom He sent? In fact, there are a lot of messages and teachings out there concerning knowing God and the Christ.

Many people are sharing their ideas and what they think concerning eternal life. I am asking what is eternal life and how do we own it? God created us as His image and likeness and He (God) breathed from His nostrils the breath of life.

Means God cause us to exist or perform like Him or to have the ability to move like Him and perform some duties as managers of creation.

Here we are already living beings out from dying or death. This means that we are to sit like Him eternally, because He breathed the breath of life into the dust He formed and the dust (Man) became a living being.

There is no way or anything which can cause or put man to death. Why because God is eternal and created an eternal thing for Himself? But what happened?

Where from dying? In fact, it is not God's intention or ever be His mind to plant a tree that can cause or put a man into death.

There is no poisonous element in the tree of knowledge of evil and of good as the Bible talks about which was in the midst of the Garden of Eden.

The fruits of that tree were not to killed or die from eating it. But the death was caused by disobediences or distrust of the word of God been command not to touch or eat from it.

The tree was to guide the continuity of the obedience to God but not to hurt man into death. God intends to maintain the faithfulness of man by the sign of that tree to keep him for imperishability or to prevent him from committing sin.

The tree was the barrier against the entry of sin and its penalties because there was an originator of sin. But man could not maintain his faithfulness to God.

This caused the death penalty and other's grief which cannot be healed by any balm or another thing except God Himself.

He planned for a man to live forever and to enjoy life throughout eternity. So far as the man cannot be redeemed by anything except by God.

The blood must be poured out or somebody must die eternally to keep a man alive continuously to pay the penalty of the sin the man has committed. By the grace and mercy of God, a second chance was given to man to stay alive forever by accepting His gift or Jesus Christ His son.

This is eternal life to know the only true God and the Son (Jesus Christ). Let's come to our question how do we know or must we know God and His son?

We have lost the character which God gave as His image and likeness and the whole nature has been turn to decay.

We have lost the glory and the covering which makes us His image and likeness. And this character needs restoration to make us fit as His image and likeness again.

To gain the image or the character of God needs total surrender of the will or be subjective to His (God) commandments.

This brings the knowledge of God into our life and makes us fit as His image not by the power or might but by His Spirit.

He created us for good works that we should give Him the glory and praise for His name sake. So, to know God means making Him do for you without your ability and will, but with your acceptance and submissive by His words.

Our whole life and everything that concerns life depend on knowing God and nothing again. You cannot know God by rejecting His single word. Many people have taken the name of Christ, but not in truth. They come near with God by their mouth but not from the true heart.

They pronounce the name of Christ, but they did not do what He says. Others praise God by their own wish and do whatever they like.

Many others sit in sin, supposing God will favor them. In fact, knowing God does not depend on our wish or how we wanted to know Him. But it depends on how we allow Him to use or control us.

This proof the genuineness's of our faith in Him. So, it is not those who say Lord; Lord are the true sons of God but those who do His will through His Spirit.

Here the true worshippers of God are those who do what God has commanded them to do by His wish, not as they wish. And this is eternal life doing what He (God) wishing you to do by His Spirit but not as you intend.

To have eternal life is to let Christ Jesus substitute your nature as His nature. Today many people go to church which belongs to wish their wish but not as the wish of God. Many others follow the tradition and instruction of man but not what God has commanded.

There are so many incidences whereby people are worshipping men and images contrary to the worship of God.

Others have formed their own righteousness to in place the righteousness of Christ Jesus. These states of worship have no position of God and cannot be accepted by Him. Let's read what the Bible is saying:

Luke 6: 46 – 49

"Why do you call me 'Lord, Lord,' and not do what I tell you? Everyone who comes to me and hears my words and does them, I will show you what he is like: he is like a man building a house, who dug deep and laid the foundation on the rock.

And when a flood arose, the stream broke against that house and could not shake it, because it had been well built. But the one who hears and does not do them is like a man who built a house on the ground without a foundation. When the stream broke against it, immediately it fell, and the ruin of that house was great."

Here, we need to consider that those who wish to live by His wish or word of God are His children. And these are the ones who know God and the Christ.

We should not deceive ourselves by doing our own wish but the wish of God. To have eternal life is to live as His words instruct us. There is no other word that can let us live apart from His word.

Note: Mathew 4:4 says; But he answered, "It is written, 'Man shall not live by bread alone, but by every word that comes from the mouth of God.'"

The word of God is our life and salvation we are to live as His word is saying; and that is eternal life. To accept Christ Jesus as your personal savior is to live as He (Christ) commanded you. In John Chapter 14: 12-15 what did Jesus said:

"Truly, truly, I say to you, whoever believes in me will also do the works that I do; and greater works than these will he do, because I am going to the Father.

Whatever you ask in my name, this I will do, that the Father may be glorified in the Son. If you ask me anything in my name, I will do it.

"If you love me, you will keep my commandments.

This is true about eternal life and there is no other thing we need to do to have eternal life, because Christ has done all for us. This is the way we know God and the Christ.

If we put God word aside we put our life aside and disrespect Him. So, there is no other thing we need to do to have eternal life but only by living according to His words instruction.

The fact is that we cannot live by His word without His power. The only thing we need to do to allow Him to lead us according to His wishes. We have no idea but only to let Him lead as it please Him.

If we seek Him; He is ready to let us find Him. Our only protection is to have the knowledge of God and it is the wall that protects us to gain the hope for eternal life. Let's consider this scripture;

Isaiah 55:6-7 says;

"Seek the Lord while he may be found; call upon him while he is near; let the wicked forsake his way, and the unrighteous man his thoughts; let him return to the Lord, that he may have compassion on him, and to our God, for he will abundantly pardon.

Many people want to seek God through others' opinion. Some also seek by the lust of flesh and what they think. But the Bible says we should seek Him by forsaken our way of life and thought. And we shall find Him that He may have compassion and abundant forgiveness. Men, the truth has been told and what will benefit us.

What we need is to allow Him to have dominion over us for salvation and everlasting peace. The way to life everlasting and certain hope is to know Him and one He sent.

John 17: 3 Says:

And this is eternal life, which they know you, the only true God, and Jesus Christ whom you have sent.

Then again John 3: 16 -18 Says:

For God so loved the world, that he gave his only Son, that whoever believes in him should not perish but have eternal life.

For God did not send his Son into the world to condemn the world, but in order that the world might be save through him.

Whoever believes in him is not condemn, but whoever does not believe is condemned already, because he has not believed in the name of the only Son of God.

The eternal life as we always seeking is based on how we will respond to His word. We have been privilege enough to have everlasting life through Christ Jesus. In fact, God has favored us and has loved us dearly that He gave His only begotten son to die for us.

Our first parents' sin was an insult to God, but He closed His eye on it and forgave us. Today we still committing the same sin even more than what our first parents did. In all, Christ has die and still advocating for us to be accepted by God.

Shall we continue doing the same as our first parents did? Many people of today think that they can be save does not matter how heavy their sin is or they can be still sinners God will save them. Let's consider this scripture:

1John 3: 9, 10 Says;

No one born of God makes a practice of sinning, for God's seed abides in him; and he cannot keep on sinning, because he has been born of God.

By this it is evident who are the children of God, and who are the children of the devil: whoever does not practice righteousness is not of God, nor is the one who does not love his brother.

We need to know that everyone born of God abides in Him and does not sin, because he is the child of God. The one who knows God does not sin but that person live as His word instructed him.

Our eternal life does not depend on the amount of words we know, but it will depend on how we live by the word whether many or little.

To know Christ or believe in Him is by doing what he says with or by His Spirit not by your wish or flesh. This is an eternal life that we live according to His word, whether many or little. What does the Scripture says?

In 1John 3: 1-3 Says:

See what kind of love the Father has given to us, that we should be called children of God; and so we are.

The reason the world does not know us is that it did not know him. Beloved, we are God's children now, and what we will be has not yet appeared; but we know that when he appears we shall be like him, because we shall see him as he is. And everyone who thus hopes in him purifies himself as he is pure.

Many people have been deceived that they can do whatever they wish; God will have mercy on them. Others says just believe in Christ and live as you desire you shall be saved. I am asking what kind of belief are they talking about?

We should not sit in sin and be proud off. We will be judged by our deeds and there will be nothing that will not be accounted.

Knowing God and the Christ whom He sent does not depend on prayers; daily or weekly worship but it depends on the acceptance of His leadership every moment on our daily life. And this is our sure of eternal life and hope of earning salvation every day. Our eternal life depends on each moment we allow Christ to lead us constantly with no acceptance of sin whether dot or large. But we must accept ourselves daily as sinners that God will have mercy upon us and to receive forgiveness. Let us know and follow His knowledge and He will come to us as a latter rain that showers the earth.

We need to understand and know that our salvation does not depend on amount of our commitment to Christ, but it will depend on how we respond to His call by His works within us. We have no way boasted of anything we can do or not. But it is by His grace that we are alive even as sinners.

Note; Thus says the Lord: "Let not the wise man boast in his wisdom, let not the mighty man boast in his might, let not the rich man boast in his richest, but let him who boasts boast in this, that he understands and knows me, that I am the Lord who practices steadfast love, justice, and righteousness in the earth. For in these things I delight, declares the Lord. Jeremiah 9:23.

This is eternal life that we may know the only true God and the Christ Jesus whom He sent. This means we must allow Him to have dominion over us and move us according to His wish. For by His grace we have been saving through faith and not by works. We are His workmanship for good works. Our hope and salvation is secured through His leadership of our being. And this is the eternal life that we may know Him and the Christ whom He sent.

5. Why are we here?

Have you ever ask yourself concerning your existence as human being and not the other creatures? Have you thought of why you are here on earth?

In fact, we have no idea concerning our existence and we cannot tell how we came about. But there is a reason why we are here on earth. Everyone has the duty and reason why we are here on earth. Let's read this scripture:

Jeremiah 1: 4, 5

Now the word of the Lord came to me, saying,

"Before I formed you in the womb I knew you,

and before you were born I consecrated you;

I appointed you a prophet to the nations."

Do you have an idea concerning our lives today on earth, but there is a purpose for us to complete or accomplish? God appointed us for a duty. It is not a mistake to be here on earth, but there is a reason. Have you asked yourself concerning the work that God has appointed you to accomplish?

What is your work now and how do you do it? What is the benefit that your work is providing? Are you honest to the work that you have been appointed? Are you selfish? How do others recognize you about your work that you are doing? How serious are you?

In fact, we are appointed by God to work for Him but not ourselves. Everyone needs to take note concerning the reason why we are alive today on earth. Why are we here? We are here for a purpose and a duty that needs completion. Many people think that they are here only for fun and selfishness.

Some also consider life as has no reason but live as you wish. Jeremiah was appointed to be the prophet for nations; to pull down and build. Means to prepare people for God and make stand perfectly before Him. It is not by accident that you are here on earth but you have been appointed for a duty.

Never live as useless being or live as you own yourself and can do whatever you wish. It is not so, but God has appointed you to work for Him concerning other people's progress. God wants you to prepare others for Him through your gift and make others survive through the work that you are doing.

Do not work as you are working for yourself but work as you have been appointed for. We are here to fulfill the mission of the owner of creation but not as we want it to be.

It is a mistake to live and work for selfish living. Many people fail concerning life matters and misuse their time for no sacrifice for others benefit.

Others abuse their gift for no improvement and die for no history activities. Do not live without good name and do not die without history of your good activities on earth. Else, you have failed to be recognized absolutely on the new earth. Everyone needs to work according to as he or she has been appointed.

Never live as without responsibility or goal but make your living meets its target. We were appointed even before been in the womb of our parents. And we were consecrated and knew by God before we were born. We are to use our talent or gift to fulfill the mission appointed by God.

Many people do not know that they have been appointed to do some specific job purposely for their fame. Others do not consider their gifts as precious but bury them through less recognition.

In fact, we cannot be anything if we put aside our gifts without using it. And it is good that we were not born than to be born for not using our gifts for owner's mission. Our mission is to fulfilling the mission of the owner through our gifts.

Moses was afraid to lead Israelites from bondage when he was appointed by God. He tried to ignore the journey to redeem Israelites from Egypt, but God instructed him to fulfill his plan.

This is the purpose of God and the purpose was to fulfill by Moses. Here Moses does not that God has appointed him to fulfill His mission before he was born. It was God's intention, but not by accident or chance.

Our talent goes with our mission and it has been planned by God not by chance but corresponding to our ability. So, we are not here as useless beings but useful beings and important managers. Our mission does not matter the age; whether child, youth or elderly.

Our goal is to fulfill the mission as soon as the life begins as human beings. Our life develops through the stages of mission progression. We should not work according to the age but should work according to the purpose set up before us.

Means we will develop through using our talents and then make differences through the age development. This makes us work perfectly and beautifully for the Master. Let's consider this scripture:

Jeremiah 1: 6-8

Then I said, "Ah, Lord God! Behold, I do not know how to speak, for I am only a youth." But the Lord said to me, "Do not say,

'I am only a youth'; for to all to whom I send you, you shall go, and whatever I command you, you shall speak. Do not be afraid of them, for I am with you to deliver you, declares the Lord."

Here, we are to be alert for the Master's mission and not to complaining about our incapability. Our duty is to accomplish the mission of the Master. Let everyone make use of his or her gift for the glory of God.

King Cyrus was appointed by God before he was born to fulfill God's mission in his time. Everyone has been appointed to work for God. We are not here just to make the earth fill with people but to work for the Master who created us.

Let's read from Isaiah 45:1- 7

Thus says the Lord to his anointed, to Cyrus, whose right hand I have grasped, to subdue nations before him and to lose the belts of kings, to open doors before him that gates may not be closed:

"I will go before you and level the exalted places, I will break in pieces the doors of bronze and cut through the bars of iron, I will give you the treasures of darkness and the hoards in secret places, that you may know that it is I, the Lord, the God of Israel, who call you by your name.

For the sake of my servant Jacob, and Israel my chosen, I call you by your name; I name you, though you do not know me.

I am the Lord, and there is no other, besides me there is no God; I equip you, though you do not know me that people may know, from the rising of the sun and from the west, that there is none besides me; I am the Lord, and there is no other. I form light and create darkness; I make well-being and create calamity; I am the Lord, who does all these things.

God has appointed us to work for Him but not for ourselves. It is God's plan for us to be here on earth but not accident or chance.

Everyone must fulfill this mission and fulfill the Master's purpose for our lives.

We are here to see God who created the heavens and earth to share the beauty of His glory. We have been invited and honored to be on earth.

We were nowhere to be found or existed. We were created from dust without hope and life. We are like dead tree or nothing to be considered. But God with His mercy and consideration with grace make us His own likeness and image.

God wants us to work with Him and join us to be in His Company as His coworkers. So, it is not our will or desire to be called by God. But it is His wish and plan to let us be in His Company as His coworkers. We have no idea and we were nothing to be recognized. So, it is not you but God who intends to make you to be with Him.

You have no word to say and have nothing to share with Him. It is His consideration and love but not beauty or anything concerning us.

Who are we to get such an opportunity to be with or called or created by God? Who can say what are you doing or question God concerning His activities?

We were created for a reason but not for anything. Everyone has work to do for the Master. We need to watch out and be careful by the way we do things.

We need to be considerate and work for the Master. We must be ready and prepare ourselves for the Master's call. Let us consider this Scripture:

Ezra 7: 10 say;

For Ezra had set his heart to study the Law of the Lord, and to do it and to teach his statutes and rules in Israel.

We have work to do and have a duty to perform. There are no reasons to question the Master or our Creator concerning our work or duty that needs accomplishment. We are His image and likeness created for His glory. We are His coworkers and loved through His mercy and grace.

We are here not to be idle but to work and progress in life. We are to work and live daily for God but not for any reason that we supposed to work for. There is no question to ask unless you do not know or maybe you need to understand some setting things.

Everyone must find out his or her talent makes use of it. We should not be useless beings but useful beings because we have the tool to work with.

It is not God's plan to create a useless thing in His creation and it has been never His plan to create something that has no duty to perform or useless thing in His creation. Note this scripture:

Proverbs 16: 4 say;

The Lord has made everything for its purpose,

even the wicked for the day of trouble.

Everything that is visible or invisible has a purpose and the reason it was created. We need to understand and know that there are no useless creatures, but useful ones and important for us to make use of it as human beings.

We have been privileged enough and honored to be His glory. Why we are here needs your attention to live and work for God. For you were created for His glory and praise.

Note: Isaiah 43:4, 7 says: Because you are precious in my eyes, and honored, and I love you, I give men in return for you, peoples in exchange for your life. everyone who is called by my name, whom I created for my glory, whom I formed and made."

We were created for His glory and honored. We need to fulfill our missions and glorify God who created us. Why are you here? We are here for a reason or purpose and it needs fulfillment. What are you doing to fulfill your goal but not as useless beings?

6. I am that I am

One day Moses led his flocks into wilderness and came to the place near the mountain of the Lord. The Angel of the Lord appeared to him in a flame of fire out of the midst of the bush.

He saw the bush burning without consuming. And Moses said, I will turn aside to see this great sight, why the bush is not burned?

When the Lord saw that he turned aside to see, God called him out of the bush and told him not to come closer to the place where the bush was burning.

According to (Exodus 3: 1- 6) when Moses heard it was God, he was afraid to look at God. This is great respecting that Moses shown to God. And God proclaim who He is to him.

Moses wanted to know more about God to make his journey successful. God made him known and pronounce His name to him. The name He gave was (I am who I am or I am that I am). What do I want you to learn?

Who knows the beginning of God and who has seen Him before? Who can describe Him or can tell His nature? The universe has the beginning and the Creator. But God is the beginner of everything. He is the first and the last. Means without Him there is no existence and there is no world. He is I am that I am!

What does I am that I am mean and why God used that name? We human beings are nothing and cannot be equal to God. But we are his image and likeness.

Let us come back to our question why God used I am that I am and what does it mean? Means He is God and there is no other. He is the beginner and the terminator of everything that exists: the seen or unseen things.

Means there is no one who can compare with. There is none like Him; all power belongs to Him, No one again. God used that name to prove His divinity and the Creator of everything.

There is no challenger or competitor who can do what He is doing. Means there is no God again.

He is I am that I am the First and the Last. He was not created by anyone or be on under somebody's hand or work under someone who is His master. He is the life and the life giver.

He is ELOHIM My Creator; He is JEHOVAH My Lord God; He is EL SHADDAI My Supplier; He is ADONAI My Master;

He is JEHOVAH JIREH My Provider; He is JEHOVAH ROPHE My Healer; He is JEHOVAH NISSI My Banner;

He is JEHOVAH MAKADESH My Sanctifier; He is JEHOVAH TSIDKENU My Righteousness; He is JEHOVAH SHALOM My Peace;

He is JEHOVAH ROHI My Shepherd; He is JEHOVAH SHAMMAH My Abiding Presence and the everlasting Father.

The real name of Lord God cannot be mention or cannot be understood or pronounce by anyone. As human beings need to fear and tremble before Him. Who are we to speak to God or have chance to come before Him? We are nothing before Him but He made us to be something and to talk to Him.

Many people do not fear God and do not want to obey His Laws and regulations. Others used His name in vain. We have cross beyond the border of our limitation. Others have taken the name of Lord into themselves which is a sin beyond the sin. No one can survive before Him even when He (God) give chance to be in His presence.

In fact, my concern of this book is to let you know who God is and why we must worship and respect Him. He is our creator and the life giver.

And we cannot be anything without Him and cannot live without Him. We need to fear and live a worthy life before Him. He is the God Almighty and we are His handy work.

Who is man that He (God) recognized him? It is His grace, mercy and love that we exist. Our lives on earth as human beings are abhorring and disgrace.

What are we doing to ourselves? In fact, we are disrespectful and do not fear God. Everyone has picked his or her own way and doing what we wish.

How can a dust stand before wind or can dust control wind? Who are we before God, the creator of the universe? Why are we so stubborn? Why do we want to live by our own wish? I am always shocked when I see men living as there are no laws or God to be respected.

We need to be careful and deeply respect the Creator of the universe and make steps as He wish us to make it. Let us consider these messages and carefully keep in mind. God created the heavens and earth in the beginning of creation. The purpose was to create the earth for a man as his eternal home.

The man was instructed and made him a manager of those creatures as we see today. As a manager on earth, the man needs to dress and to keep the land. Here, the man became the manager or the caretaker of a house. The Owner of the house showed him everything.

He was instructed to eat freely from the trees that bear fruits in the premises of the house. But he was forbidden to eat from a setting tree in the midst of the house managing. As a manager and caretaker he must obey his master's instruction. But the man could not obey what he was instructed with.

Moreover, he obeyed to a certain stubborn servant who could not maintain his dignity as a servant of the same Owner of the house. Here, I want you to follow me well concerning this message and know how stubborn we are in the world today. How can a servant live as he wishes in his master's house but not as the master's wish or instruction?

How can a dead tree talk to a living tree? How can a stranger know more than the ruler of the city? How can a dust control the wind? How can a man teach God what to do or instruct Him the way He should go? Who are we to say to God what are you doing? In fact, we have sin above the sin and have gone beyond the boundary.

Why many people wants to live as they wish but not as the Master's wishes? He is the Alpha and Omega, the First and the Last. We are nothing before Him and cannot be something before Him. But He makes us to be something by His own wish through His own choice. And He made us to be useful by His own mercy and grace.

I am that I am as a title of this book is to let you know who God is and how we must fear and respect deeply than what it must be before. We cannot teach God in anything and cannot instruct Him concerning anything! How can we question God on His doings or give Him an opinion?

He is (JEHOVAH JIREH) our provider and the life giver. Without Him we are nothing and cannot be anything without His choice. How must we live before Him and what is our duty? How must we work and act in His presence?

We are the managers of His creation. In fact, God intends to create a man to act in His behalf on earth. The earth was made for Adam as his eternal home.

He was ordained to have dominion over every creature on this earth. So, he was created like God Himself on this earth to be the ruler of this earth not as to be worship like God, but to be the ruler and the manager for eternity on this earth.

A man was highly honored with all the abilities necessary for his progress. He was perfectly made and lacks nothing necessary for his life journey. In other words, the earth was to be the second home for God ruling by a man (Adam). The earth was totally made for a man and it is his gift eternally. But he was not the owner but manager.

When someone gives you something to keep and manage that doesn't mean it is you who own it. But you have to account for it. As a manager of creatures, his work is to manage according to regulation. He should not go beyond the guideline. The one who gave you the gift needs your respect and appreciation.

Why all these comments? God needs to be respected and honored. He is the creator of the universe and everything concerning us. But what are we doing to ourselves and the world today? The world is confused and there is no peace, everyone do what his or her wishes.

We have gone beyond the demarcation and have reach beyond shame. Women wear what they like and men take women in abundant without considering of the law. Others eat as to their wish but not as required.

Many people make money unlawful way and others bribe and kill innocent people. There are many false teachers and prophets seeking money aggressively with their lies prophecies. Others are confused and do not know what to do in life.

Corruption and bribery are now capital for job creation. Lies have now become the keys that open success of life and the truth has been tremble on the ground.

Men have forgotten the creator and the life giver of the universe. We have lost our identity and the character which belongs to us. We have turned our back towards heaven and front towards hell.

Our mind has become dark and the thoughts are always evil. Men find it difficult to tell the truth than to tell the lies. We have lost our dignity and fame as human beings.

We all have gone astray and have put God aside seeking for money than life eternal. We have broken the law and have thrown our dignity aside.

One day God appears to Abraham and said walk before me and be perfect (Genesis 17:1). We must walk before God and be blameless; why because He is God Almighty and our Creator. In fact, we have put the fear of God aside as human beings and join hands with the devil to oppose God in all our doings.

As our maker and the life giver He (God) needs our deep respect and praise from us! He wasn't created by anyone and do not depend on anyone to survive. He is I am who I am, the maker and the life giver. Isaiah saw God and was afraid to look at Him.

(Isaiah) 6:1 - 6 let's read:

In the year that King Uzziah died I saw the Lord sitting upon a throne, high and lifted up; and the train of his robe filled the temple. Above him stood the seraphim.

Each had six wings: with two he covered his face, and with two he covered his feet, and with two he flew. And one called to another and said: "Holy, holy, holy is the Lord of hosts; the whole earth is full of his glory!"

And the foundations of the thresholds shook at the voice of him who called, and the house was filled with smoke. And I said: "Woe is me! For I am lost; for I am a man of unclean lips, and I dwell in the midst of a people of unclean lips; for my eyes have seen the King, the Lord of hosts!"

Then one of the seraphim flew to me, having in his hand a burning coal that he had taken with tongs from the altar. And he touched my mouth and said: "Behold, this has touched your lips; your guilt is taken away, and your sin atoned for."

We need to fear God and honor Him! He is our source of life and provider. He is everything, and He is everything that we need. Why because it is He who created everything.

We did not need everything but we need God because He made all things whether great or small; whether Spirit or flesh, whether good or bad.

He created everything for His glory and fame. He is I am that I am and the everlasting Father. He needs to be fear and worship! Let's consider these scriptures:

Isaiah 42:5 - 9

Thus says God, the Lord, who created the heavens and stretched them out, who spread out the earth and what comes from it, who gives breath to the people on it and spirit to those who walk in it: "I am the Lord; I have called you in righteousness;

I will take you by the hand and keep you; I will give you as a covenant for the people, a light for the nations, to open the eyes that are blind, to bring out the prisoners from the dungeon, from the prison those who sit in darkness.

I am the Lord; that is my name; my glory I give to no other, nor my praise to carved idols. Behold, the former things have come to pass, and new things I now declare; before they spring forth I tell you of them."

Isaiah 43: 9-13 Says: "You are my witnesses," declares the Lord, "and my servant whom I have chosen, that you may know and believe me and understand that I am he. Before me no god was formed, nor shall there be any after me.

I, I am the Lord, and besides me there is no savior. I declared and saved and proclaimed, when there was no strange god among you; and you are my witnesses," declares the Lord, "and I am God. Also henceforth I am he; there is none who can deliver from my hand; I work, and who can turn it back?"

What are we doing to ourselves on this earth before God? Shall we not fear and tremble? Who are we before God and what do we want to do before Him? There is no god formed before Him and there shall be no any after Him. He is the Lord and besides Him there is no savior. As managers of His creation, we need to be honest and be blameless before Him.

Isaiah 48:12, 13 says:

"Listen to me, O Jacob, and Israel, whom I called! I am he; I am the first, and I am the last. My hand laid the foundation of the earth, and my right hand spread out the heavens; when I call to them, they stand forth together.

This is the Lord I am talking about and you did not need to teach above or contrary to this God that I am writing about him. But what I want you know is to fear and give glory to HIM!

For His judgment is near and worship Him who made the Heavens and the Earth; the spring of water and everything that eye can see or not, ear can hear or not! Be on your feet and do the right thing before God.

For He is I am that I am! That is, He shall continue as He is through eternity and does not change. He is I am who I am!

7. The Love of God

Who can describe the beauty of God's love or who can explain to the deepest of God's attitude towards human beings? Is there anything that is greater than the love of God? Who can totally understand the love of God? What is this love?

As the Owner and creator of the universe, He (God) creates an image resemblance to Himself and acting according to His likeness. God did everything that is needed for the image He made.

It is not by mistake but by intention to make someone live like Him. So, He formed the dust from the ground and made it like Himself and breathes the breath of life from His nostrils and that image He formed became a living being.

He taught him everything needed to be educating with and honored him more than the other creatures. He (God) instructed him to trust His word to be obedient to that. The man owns everything, and he is the manager who controls and make use of the surrounding creatures.

But he was forbidden eat from the tree in the midst of the place that the man lives. But man could not obey the words of God concerning not to eat from that tree.

The man distrusted the word of God and he did his wish but not what God wishes. But with all this stubbornness, God makes a way for man to live again and restored him to his office.

There was a death penalty for a man when he distrusts the word of God. It is a rightful way to get forgiveness of sin when the blood was poured. So, God killed the lamb to make the man received the forgiveness of sin by His own love. The man was intentionally done wrong to God and distrusted His word.

But God with His mercy and love closed His eyes on it and forgave. How can we understand this love and what it is about? Is there anything which can compare with God's love for us?

Who can exchange his or her life for someone else? Or stand to die for somebody he does not know him and deserve to die for his sin?

We are sinners and deserve to die for the sins we have committed. Adam committed sin with his children and his children became sinners even when they are not yet born.

For all have sin and have fall short of the glory of God. (Romans 3:23). In fact, we deserve to die eternally because of the sin committed against God. Why because we insulted our Creator and distrust his words.

We have no excuse and have no answer to our sins. But God with His mercy and grace considered us again carried the sin to Himself as the one who has committed the sin and death for it. This is the love of God for us given Jesus Christ to die for us. He was placed in our place as a sinner and die for it instead of us.

We cannot explain this kind of love and cannot know the reason of such love; because it is not possible for a master to die for a servant who has committed a grievous sin or sleep outside for a servant to sleep in his bedroom for the sake of his own merit. I want you to know more about the love of God and His consideration towards us.

Who are we and what is our value? We are dust and are nothing to be use for something. How can we exchange a precious thing for a dust which cannot be use for anything? With all our conditions, God did not look at it but considered and exchange His precious son for a dust (Man) or us. But God shows His love for us in that while we were still sinners, Christ died for us. (Romans 5:8).

Let us think of this statement and consider the question I am about to ask. One day a dog took somebody's meat and the man whose meat was taken by the dog pointed a gun on the dog and tempted to kill it.

But a setting man suddenly came and said kill me and leave the dog to go free. Instantly the man whose meat was stolen by the dog killed the man who devoted his life for the dog; and the dog fleet as was told by the devotee.

Everyone who heard was amaze about that incident. How can a man devoted to die for a dog? This is what Jesus did for us and there is no greatest love than this; that someone will die for his friends. In John 15: 13 says; Greater love has no one than this, that someone lay down his life for his friends.

Christ has redeemed us, by which we have no idea. We need to consider this act very carefully and be thankful every day. God loves us so much that He exchanges His life for us. Moreover, there is nothing again that is needful in our life than his love for us.

We must think of it every day that He is ready for all our needs. We need not to fear of needs and do not worry about tomorrow. For if He did not spare his son but gave Him up for us, how can He freely not give us all things.

Who can condemn us? It is Christ who die for us and has risen from death and interceding for us. Let us read this text:

John 3:16 says;

("For God so loved the world, that he gave his only Son, that whoever believes in him should not perish but have eternal life)

Verse 17 says; For God did not send his Son into the world to condemn the world, but in order that the world might be saved through him.

Upon all our sins, God loves us and He has not condemned us. We are highly favored and esteemed by God. It is God's will to be with Him in Paradise and stay eternally like Him! It is also God intention to be on earth again eternally as He did at the beginning. In fact, no one can explain the love of God towards us.

The love of God towards us cannot be explain by any language even Heaven Angel do not understand such a love. God has make away by which we might have eternal life. All His doings are towards our salvation. It is God's will that none of us shall perish but to have eternal life.

Jesus wants us to live, and it is His will to die even eternally for us to live eternally! That is why He dies on the cross for our sins. Let us consider this statement:

Our nature as human beings today is meaningless and it cannot be meaningful without Christ. We are not as what God wishes to work with; and we have lost the state that is meaningful to Him.

Our nature today has lost the glory of God and there is nothing with us that He can wish to make Him complete as God. That is, we are not complete as to let God enjoy with us.

We have totally lost His image and likeness. Means we have die to talk with by sin and have become useless more than first dust He used to create us.

We have been decay and corrupted by disobedient and there is nothing with us that makes God happy. We are no more God likeness and image for His glory; we have been deformed by sin. But with all these conditions, God intended to restore and make us honorable again.

Moreover, there is nothing that can restore us to the first state, unless someone wishes to die eternally for us. And there is no one who can pay the price or redeem us from such a condition more worthy than the price! So, it's took God Himself to pay for it.

We have been redeemed by God's blood and it is His blood only that can pay the price but no other. How can we redeem by God's blood? Who are we? It's took God's life to makes our lives dear to Him. Means, there is nothing that can pay the price except God.

This is the love of God; it cost him to sacrifices Himself to make us well before Him! Oh my dear! What again do we need or what is our problem that God does not mind? The amount of goodness which the whole human race can show to God cannot be anything concerning what God through Christ has done for us.

This is more than a precious thing or anything concerning treasured! We need not worry or think to lose our life unless we disregard God's love for us. He has done everything which needs to be done for our salvation. Who are we that God love us so much? Let us read this scripture:

Romans 8:31-39.

What then shall we say to these things? If God is for us, who can be against us? He who did not spare his own Son but gave him up for us all, how will he not also with him graciously give us all things? Who shall bring any charge against God's elect? It is God who justifies.

Who is to condemn? Christ Jesus is the one who died—more than that, who was raised—who is at the right hand of God, who indeed is interceding for us. Who shall separate us from the love of Christ?

Shall tribulation, or distress, or persecution, or famine, or nakedness, or danger, or sword? As it is written,

"For your sake we are being killed all the day long; we are regarded as sheep to be slaughtered." No, in all these things we are more than conquerors through him who loved us.

For I am sure that neither death nor life, nor angels nor rulers, nor things present nor things to come, nor powers, nor height nor depth, nor anything else in all creation, will be able to separate us from the love of God in Christ Jesus our Lord.

We have no idea concerning this love and chance that God have shown to us. And we cannot answer, if we disregard this love of God. It will be a hell, if we dash this love on our foot. Means making this love of God a fruitless for our life! It is impossible for us to lose or separate from the love of God towards us, unless we make it void.

This is the inheritance of the children of God that no weapon can stand against us in judgment. Christ is the one who die for us. Who shall bring any charge against God's elect? It is God who justifies.

We have been given chance and opportunities likely to be accepted by God. There is no doubt about it our life is certain in Christ and has been sealed if we continue to make Him Lord in our life.

If we reject Him, He will reject us. If we embrace with Him, He will surely embrace with us. God is love and His love does not cease even when we are on our graves.

We dear to Him and shall be dear to Him eternally. He punishes us through His love and teaches us by His love. What must we do or how shall we respond to His love towards us? Let us note this scripture in Hebrews 2:1-4, 8, 9 says;

Therefore we must pay much closer attention to what we have heard, lest we drift away from it. For since the message declared by angels proved to be reliable, and every transgression or disobedience received a just retribution, how shall we escape if we neglect such a great salvation?

It was declared at first by the Lord, and it was attested to us by those who heard, while God also bore witness by signs and wonders and various miracles and by gifts of the Holy Spirit distributed according to his will. Putting everything in subjection under his feet."

Now in putting everything in subjection to him, he left nothing outside his control. At present, we do not yet see everything in subjection to him.

But we see him who for a little while was made lower than the angels, namely Jesus, crowned with glory and honor because of the suffering of death, so that by the grace of God he might taste death for everyone.

Christ, taste death for us and there is nothing again that is more or greater than what He did for us. He loves us even to death, for He wishes us to live by His death and wishes to die eternally for us even if He could not resurrected again. Have you imagined such a love before or are you now want to think off?

This is the love of God shown to us! We should not worry concerning what we will eat or cloth or sleep. Our situations are dear is to Him, and He will provide all our needs even if He must die for it.

Here, Christ paid the price by His blood to redeem us from the second death or the eternal death. He was killed for our sin penalty and has resurrected for all our needs. He is alive to advocate for us.

Isaiah 53:10 says: Yet it was the will of the Lord to crush him; he has put him to grief; when his soul makes an offering for guilt, he shall see his offspring; he shall prolong his days; the will of the Lord shall prosper in his hand.

We human beings sin against God at the beginning of our existence. We insulted our Creator and distrusted His words. The sin that was committed by our first parents was more than a curse.

This causes the unhealed decay to all human beings and there is no other thing that can solve this situation. But God took the cost to Himself, pay the price and bear the punishment.

Let us consider this act of God and cherish it! For He loves us and wants our wellbeing. Men let us love, for God is love! Note 1John 3:1-3 says:

See what kind of love the Father has given to us, that we should be called children of God; and so we are. The reason why the world does not know us is that it did not know him.

Beloved, we are God's children now, and what we will be has not yet appeared; but we know that when he appears we shall be like him, because we shall see him as he is. And everyone who thus hopes in him purifies himself as he is pure.

The love of God cannot cease and it is new every day great is His faithfulness. God has akin us to Himself and suffered for sin punishment for us. He bears the cross and shame for us and pays the price which no blood can pay for.

How must we respond to this love? We are His bride and everything He loves us and we are dear to Him even than Himself. Let us consider and do something that will show our appreciation towards what He has done to us!

8. Why we must Fear God?

He created the world out of nothing and there were no existence of anything. We have no idea of the creation and where God comes from or how He came to be. He is the Alpha and Omega! All things come by Him and all things shall go through Him.

The sea and the other waters are called by God's word. In the beginning God created the Heavens and the earth. Here God already exists before he planned of this creation that we are part as His managers. We have no idea and we cannot tell how we are here today on this earth.

We need to fear and mind our words and steps. In the beginning was the word and the word was with God and the word was God. All things were created through Him and without Him was nothing that was made. He was in the world and the world was made through Him.

The world was created by the word of God and there was nothing that does not come by the word of God. All things were made through His word. Who can tell how God created this world by His words? Who can describe how the nature came out? We have no idea and we cannot say anything concerning it. How it was all began?

Even Angels cannot describe or explain to us how it was all started. Who are we and what do we know? We have gone beyond the boundary and have insulted God through our actions and conduct.

We need consider whatever we are doing before God and we need to fear before Him. Means we must act careful before Him and respect deeply.

Let us consider those things around us; that is our environment or things around us. Have we had any idea about the things around us and how it performs? Can we create one tree or any of the animals that live together with us?

Who created all these things that we see and used of them? Who can tell how we became human beings? Who can count the hair of our heads?

Who can tell the side of the sea and the earth? Who can tell the depth of the sea? How did earth come about? With all these questions I have asked, who can answer truly?

We were nowhere and cannot tell how we became human beings. Who are we before God? In fact, I want you to think and consider your act before God and this earth.

We must know how to deal with God excellently and carefully because He is our Creator. The Heaven declares the glory of God and the sky above proclaims His handiwork.

All things work according to how God has commanded it work. There are no voices which can be heard or talks that are commanding but all things do His wishes.

Day to day pours out a speech, and night to night reveals knowledge. The world and everything in them educate us about the one who created them. Everything that God created has its purpose and the benefit to mankind. The world has abundant resources and many other things necessary for man's aid.

God created everything for the man's sake and nothing was left which will be needed for his lives. God love us so much that even He planned not to lose us when we commit sin. We are His love and everything.

He devoted His time and life for our sake and for His glory sake. He makes everything for us to prove His love for us. He planned to die for us as soon as we commit sin to have us again.

Through His love for us, He designed night and day to keep our fitness and consider our health by given us work to do. Who are we that God love us so much?

He designed us to be creators like Him and furnished us as His image and likeness. We need not to fear for wants and worrying about life that is set before us. We must trust Him and His words to us. We must fear and tremble before Him!

He created us not to be speechless but He allows us to speak to Him. He did not condemn us when we sin but comfort us by His word and forgive when we confess.

We are His dear creature amongst the creatures. He loves us and has good plans for our future. Let us read this scripture: Isaiah 40:27-31 says:

Why do you say, O Jacob, and speak, O Israel, "My way is hidden from the Lord, and my right is disregarded by my God"? Have you not known? Have you not heard? The Lord is the everlasting God, the Creator of the ends of the earth. He does not faint or grow weary; his understanding is unsearchable.

He gives power to the faint, and to him who has no might he increases strength. Even youths shall faint and be weary, and young men shall fall exhausted; but they who wait for the Lord shall renew their strength; they shall mount up with wings like eagles; they shall run and not be weary; they shall walk and not faint.

We are not absent before God but we are always present before Him. The youth shall faint and be weary but they that wait upon the Lord shall renew their strength and mount up like eagles and shall walk and not be faint.

We must keep on trusting God for He can do all things and keep us alive even when we are in danger. Our ways are not hidden from the Lord and our rights are regarded by Him.

We are honored and love by God and we should not fear for He is always with us. We have been engraved on the palms of the Lord and our walls are always before Him.

He always remembering us and we are not forsaken. He wants our best and we are precious before Him. If we look at our situation today on this earth, we can see that our lives are always at risk. Our hopes have lost and we fear for wants and death. We need not to be worry and fear wants.

God is always near to help; He is the friend indeed for the time of needs. He created all things and everything is for Him.

What we need to do is to fear; respect and obey what He is saying to us. He loves us and wants us good forever! We need to fear God because He is our creator and life giver.

9. God Intention for Man

Oh, my dear! Can you imagine how God's love you and the plans He has for you? It is not the plan of evil but of peace; expectation and the great future. We were created for His glory and we are His image and resemblance. God created us as Himself and want best for us as to Himself.

It is His (God) intention to let us enjoy life eternally and do ourselves good of His wishes. The higher than the highest thought that human can reach is the God's ideal for a man. It is His desire to make us like Him again and be with Him forever.

In fact, God design this world for us and it is His intention to let us own it forever and to develop to the highest peak. He created us like Him and in other words, to act and do things like Him on this earth.

He gave us will to make a choice for our own; means He allows us to do for ourselves but not to move and act like a robot as it has being program by Him.

But He gave us ability to think; to create and to plan by doing other things through knowledge and sensitivity He has given to us.

It is not God wish to control our choice or will, but it is His will to allow Him to be our coworker in whatever we want to do. He does not force us to do His will, but it is our duty to do His will, because He is our Creator.

Here shows the kind of God He is; that is why He is I am that I am. He does not change and cannot be change from His love for us. One thing we need to know and understand is that we were created for His glory.

So, we are His fame and greatness to prove His power and ability. So far as we are His fame, He is working every day and night for our progress.

The world has been corrupted by sin and the activities of men. But God is in control to keep and protect from total damage.

Our ways are not His ways and our thoughts are not His thoughts. He wants our peace and future hope. For His name sake and our sake, He does not leave us alone, but He is always with us to help.

It is God purpose that we become like Him and live forever. We were created not to die but to be active for eternity.

Upon all that has come to us as human beings; God is still working to have us back as it was at the beginning. He knows the thoughts that He is thinking towards us; the thoughts of peace but not of evil.

God wants our progress and want our best than the best. He wants our fame for His name sake. We should not worry about tomorrow and what we can be; it is God concern and His work but not us. What we need to do is to trust Him and continue on what we are doing.

God wants us to reach a higher standard; to be pure, noble and good. We need not to complain every day and shift blame to others who did not do their part.

But rather, seek God and His kingdom for all things will add unto you. Means you would not lack anything in life but rather all things will work together for your good. Let consider this text from Isaiah chapter 52:1, 2 says

Awake, awake, put on your strength, O Zion; put on your beautiful garments, O Jerusalem, the holy city; for there shall no more come into you the uncircumcised and the unclean.

Shake yourself from the dust and arise; be seated, O Jerusalem; loose the bonds from your neck, O captive daughter of Zion.

God want us to come out from our weakness and put on our strength and beautiful garment. And break out from sin bondage and shake ourselves from dust. Means we should awake from our slumber and be alert for good works.

He is willing to help and establish us again. In fact, we should not overwhelm by what we eat and wear, but we must seek and allow God to do for us.

We have been redeemed by the blood of Christ Jesus and there is nothing that God will withhold from giving to us. It is His intention to let us enjoy the best of the best and the most among the most. To be God on the earth and rule as his kingdom and eternal home forever and ever.

Moreover, we are His self-image and the glory of His creative art honored by life and everything that is needful to live with. We are not mere beings but higher and cherish by the Creator Himself.

He crowned us with precious things that will make Him enjoy with us. So, if God created us as His image, what then do we need again?

There is no honor that supersede this type of endowment that God did for man. That is, to be His image and likeness. What is my whole idea of this content? In fact, I want you to know who God is and what He wants you to be.

There is no doubt, God loves us and want our best more than what we thought off. We are the product of God for a price that money cannot pay for but His life and blood.

He wants us to be hopeful; we are not abandoned or rejected; for He has loved us with an everlasting love, that is why He has love us with loving kindness and everlasting.

Note, to your old age I will carry you in my shoulders and will not forget you. You are always at His presence and we are engraved in His palms, our walls are always before Him. He is with us until the end of the age.

We are His glory and His self-image made to be glorifying His name sake. He loves us and cherishes our life and wants us to gain His character again. What do we need again?

10. Never take God Less

Who can find out God and who has been His counselor? We human beings do not fear God and do not respect Him at all! Many people think that God is good and cannot harm us.

Others too think that God is too slow to revenge, and the foolish think that there is no God at all. Who created the Heavens and the earth and you who dwell on this earth? Where from those things we see or how do they survive?

Who can survive in the presence of God or stand before Him? Who are you to live and joke before God on this earth? Moses could not look at Him when he first heard of His voice and bow down before Him. Let us consider ourselves well in act; in speech and in all our doings before God.

He is a consuming fire and the revenger of our deeds. It is very difficult to understand God and know His ways concerning us. We are His creatures and His glory which define His power or might. We should not take God less or think that He does not mean what He says.

The world has the beginnings and the things that are in them testify the one who created it. Are we not fear and tremble before Him? How do we want to live in this world? Why we are not feared before God? Why do we want to live anyhow on this earth? God is present everywhere, and He sees everything.

He knows our thoughts and foreseen our acts. There is nothing that can be hidden from Him. He knew us before we were born and know what we will be at the end. There is nothing that is new to Him and there will be nothing without Him. Means He created everything and all things comes by Him.

He is omnipresent and a supreme being. He was not created by anyone and there is none to teach Him something. He can die and resurrected by Himself. He can become anything and can be nothing and something at any time. Means you cannot compare anything with Him that can be equal with Him.

God is wonderful to describe or explain. We have no idea with Him and we cannot find out and understand Him. He knows the volume of the sea and amount of it sand. He knows every bird and their number. He has count the hair of heads and knows every organ of our being.

He knows every particle that forms the earth and the amount of it. He has named every tree and knows their number. There is that comes in and out without His permission. He owns the Heavens and the earth. Who can hide before God or can escape His judgment or can run before Him?

His voice is like many waters and His brightness is stronger than the sun more than seven times. Who can stand before Him and be alive? He remembers everything that His has created at the same time and knows the number of each.

Who are we that He remembered us? Or even to call His Name? He is I AM, and He is still I AM. His ways are not our ways and our thoughts are not His thoughts.

As the Heavens are higher than the earth, so are His ways greater than our ways; also concerning His thoughts and everything greater than ours.

We need to fear and tremble before Him. God is good and wicked at some time; why because He can destroy and rebuild at the same time. It is fearful to fall in the hands of the Lord. Let us read Hebrews 10:26-31

For if we go on sinning deliberately after receiving the knowledge of the truth, there no longer remains a sacrifice for sins, but a fearful expectation of judgment, and a fury of fire that will consume the adversaries.

Anyone who has set aside the Law of Moses dies without mercy on the evidence of two or three witnesses. How much worse punishment, do you think, will be deserved by the one who has trampled underfoot the Son of God, and has profaned the blood of the covenant by which he was sanctified, and has outraged the Spirit of grace?

For we know him who said, "Vengeance is mine; I will repay." And again, "The Lord will judge his people." It is a fearful thing to fall into the hands of the living God.

One thing we need to know is that it is God who vengeance is for Him; and it is fearful to fall in His hands. We need to behaviour well on this earth and act according to the rules that govern it as established by God. We have gone beyond the margin and have broken the covenant between us and God.

He is our creator and life giver. We should not take God less but to take Him serious and fear. We must walk before Him and be perfect; let consider our ways and acts then move as His wishes us. For we know Him who said vengeance is mine and I will repay.

The Lord will judge His people and it is a fearful thing to fall into the hands of the living God. Many people today have taken sin like food eating it day and night.

Others think that there is no punishment if you commit sin. In the olden days, when someone breaks the Law of Moses in the camp of Israel, that person dies without mercy by two or three witnesses.

How much worse punishment do you think, will be deserved by someone who has trampled underfoot the son of God and has profaned the blood of the covenant?

What God has done for us cannot be margin, and there is nothing that can be comparing with or to have the same cost like that.

We must value it and take a look at each minute; then behavior well and act according to the price paid. Shall we not fear before the Lord our maker?

Shall we continue in stubbornness of our heart and sin against God? Men, do not take God less but fear Him and be watchful of your doings. He never slumbers or sleeps; He does not become weak or grow old. He is the same yesterday, today and forevermore.

He did everything through love and wishes to make us dear. We need to fear and honor Him; for He loves us and care for us; we are not alone; He is always with and will be with us until the end of the world.

Our God is a consuming fire and His name is I am that I am and the almighty God. Let us to the throng of grace and receive mercy in the time of need. We need to picture how great He is and know how to walk before Him.

Take note in Revelation 4:1-6 and see the one who created us and then fear and respect Him deeply. Read;

After these things I looked, and behold, a door standing open in heaven. And the first voice which I heard was like a trumpet speaking with me, saying, "Come up here, and I will show you things which must take place after this."

2Immediately I was in the Spirit; and behold, a throne set in heaven, and One sat on the throne. 3And He who sat there was like a jasper and a sardius stone in appearance; and there was a rainbow around the throne, in appearance like an emerald.

4Around the throne were twenty-four thrones, and on the thrones I saw twenty-four elders sitting, clothed in white robes; and they had crowns of gold on their heads.

5And from the throne proceeded lightnings, thunderings, and voices. Seven lamps of fire were burning before the throne, which are the seven Spirits of God.

6Before the throne there was a sea of glass, like crystal. And in the midst of the throne, and around the throne, were four living creatures full of eyes in front and in back.

John saw unapproachable lightnings and thunderings and one who was like a jasper and a sardius stone in appearance. Before Him there was living creatures full of eyes in front and in back. There was a sea of glass like a crystal and the thrones around Him.

Moses and other prophets like Daniel saw this seen but could not observed. Who are we? He is siting between Cherubim, perfect and unstained beings are before Him praising and adore Him day and night without rest.

Do you not fear and tremble before Him. The Bible says the Lord is in His temple let all the earth be silent before Him.

God is a dreadful and mysterious with clouds; darkness and light, very wonderful to describe. We need not to take Him less for we are His creature made by His image and likeness. Have you considered? Do you not fear and be tremble before Him?

11. Who can stand?

The world was created out of nothing by God; He is the author and finisher of our fate. He began everything or matters of this world. In the beginning God created the Heavens and the earth, and the earth was formless and void. That is, without production or a living and non-living thing. Means there was no matter which can be used for anything.

It was a vacuum space and hollow. The world at that time was nothing; means it does not have any identification to describe it. It was a meaningless thing and it cannot be useful. But God makes it a useful thing and dress it with useful ingredients. He expanded it and gathers the waters into one place. There were no living things and other beings.

In fact, we cannot tell how it came to be and cannot explain the deeper meaning concerning all creation. It is God who can explain and where this world came from.

We do not know how and cannot have a word to say about it. The world was darkness and there was no light. The whole place was filled with waters and God's Spirit was moving over the space of waters.

Here God did something; He modifies the state of this world by His word. In all, there was a purpose for doing that. He filled the earth with different ingredients and resources.

He intentionally did this to make it useful by someone. In the process of time, He made things sequentially to suit the beauty that He needs for someone. Moreover, the intention was achieved, and all things intended for were very good.

With six days He achieved His goal and did something different from the creation. He rested on the seventh day and sanctifies it. Means no work was done in the seventh day. God set it apart to be His sign or seal of His creation. It is God's idea to make the seventh day a day for serving Him.

For in the six days, God created the Heavens and the earth and rested on the seventh day. The seventh day is the seal of God's creation and it is a sign of His identity as the creator of the Heavens and the earth. If you disregard the seventh day, you disregard God as the maker of the universe. We need to take note and observe the seventh day as sanctify by God.

Furthermore, God created a man (male and female) in His image and resemblance. He designed and built an apartment for the man and surrounded him, all the necessary things need for his movement. He instructed him to till the land and dress it. To keep and to care for all things that have been created.

The world was created for a man to be the ruler of all things that move upon the face of it. The man has no idea how he came and cannot tell which transpired. He was perfect and handsome; fit and capable with all the ideas meant to do.

God created raw materials for the man to make use of it by his own wish. Means, God did not create a man to be idle but to use his ability for development. It is God's idea to make a man progress through activities of his skills.

He instructed him by the way he should go and last as his creator. The man was the crown being and the ruler of all the creatures of the earth. He was perfect and God resemblance, fit and energetic.

There was no disease or sickness or wound of anything that were created for a man. Peace prevail and everything were good and calm in it state. There was no condition of fear of wants and failed.

The world was comfort and fun to live; the joy was everywhere in the globe. There was no death or cry anywhere on the globe. Adam and his wife enjoyed the best at the beginning. Why are we suffering today?

Where from dying? What has happened? The man disobeyed his master's instruction and distrusted His word. This caused the death penalty to man and all his children which will be after him.

Who can stand and what will be our last penalty? There was a price that needs payment and the price was too heavy for a man to be paid. So, God intend to pay the price by Himself. It cost His life to pay this price that man has invented.

There was no other thing that can pay this price, except blood that is free from sin. There wasn't any means to solve this problem. This death penalty was a second death; means to die for eternity. Christ accepted this death for man and die for him. In fact, it was a grave decision that He made and suffered for it.

Here, punishment and death has been taken from man if he accepts that death of Christ. But how can we escape, if we neglect this death of Christ?

Let's come back to our content; who can stand? We have no idea of our creation and the love shown to us by Christ's death.

If God Himself have die because of our sins committed by our first parents; (innocently) what will be the punishment of the one who committed it? Shall we continue disobeying His instruction?

There is no remission of sin if we continuing in sin deliberately after haven the knowledge of truth. There left the fearful judgment that will consume the adversaries. God is coming pay back or revenge on the sin committed against Him.

He is coming with the Heavenly Angels and with His reward to give to each one according to his work done. The mountains run before Him and the earth cannot stay quietly before Him.

Repent for the Kingdom of God is at hand; come you that labor and have heavy laden, I will give you rest. It is fast for you to go into sin than to going to good.

Who are you oh man that can stand before God? Let's consider our state and the condition of the God's judgment. Is there anything that we can do about it? How can we escape this judgment?

Note the words of Christ; "For God so loved the world, that he gave his only Son, that whoever believes in him should not perish but have eternal life.

For God did not send his Son into the world to condemn the world, but in order that the world might be saved through him. Whoever believes in him is not condemned, but whoever does not believe is condemned already, because he has not believed in the name of the only Son of God.

And this is the judgment: the light has come into the world, and people loved the darkness rather than the light because their works were evil. For everyone who does wicked things hates the light and does not come to the light, lest his works should be exposed.

But whoever does what is true comes to the light, so that it may be clearly seen that his works have been carried out in God."(John 3:16-21)

The one who believe the son of God will be escape condemnation. But the one who does not believe in Him will be condemned. We have no excuse and cannot have an answer for our sins; if we disregard to confess and repent from it. Christ has done a lot for us and has loved us even into death.

What is our appreciation to Him? We need to be appreciating Him for what has done for us. Make Him feel good each day and night by accepting His ruler-ship in our life.

It is His wish that we will have life abundantly. He loves us and wishes best of life and reasonable ends. God hate sin and hate disobedient and love those who keep His Laws and eschew evil doing.

We cannot stand before Him if we continue in our evil deeds. God killed Nadab and Abihu through disobedient. Everyone who comes to Lord must be careful and him or herself well before the Lord.

When Moses was leading Israel some centuries ago, the Lord instructed him concerning their presentation before Him; that they should act holy and eschew evil in His presence and in all their camps.

They should wash themselves and avoid evil doing. Aaron and sons must be holy and act decently before Him.

We cannot be accepted by God when intend to do evil or agree with other foreign matters contrary to His principles. The priest was instructed not to drink any wine or any substance that is an intoxicating drink.

Lest they will die and this was instituted throughout their generation. Why these comments? We cannot stand before God with any dot or jot of sin when He appears the second time of His coming. We must eschew evil today and live according to His principles.

No one can escape His judgment or death sentence that is before us. Who can stand before the coming judgment? Oh, my dear! Is there anyone who is important than Christ who dies on the cross? Or do you have anyone who can do than Christ? Or do you have someone who is life giver than Christ? Is there any god who can rescue you from the coming judgment day?

The day will come which no one can survive and there are other things that will happen before the coming of the son of man that will be terrible.

Who knows the evil hour or who can describe the condition in which this world will go through? Let's consider these incidences and know how we will live our life. Let's reads some quotes from Revelation:

Chapter 14:9-11

9Then a third angel followed them, saying with a loud voice, "If anyone worships the beast and his image, and receives his mark on his forehead or on his hand,

10he himself shall also drink of the wine of the wrath of God, which is poured out full strength into the cup of His indignation. He shall be tormented with fire and brimstone in the presence of the holy angels and in the presence of the Lamb.

11And the smoke of their torment ascends forever; and they have no rest day or night, who worship the beast and his image, and whoever receives the mark of his name."

Chapter 16:1-6

Then I heard a loud voice from the temple saying to the seven angels, "Go and pour out the bowls of the wrath of God on the earth." 2So the first went and poured out his bowl upon the earth, and a foul and loath some sore came upon the men who had the mark of the beast and those who worshiped his image.

3Then the second angel poured out his bowl on the sea, and it became blood as of a dead man; and every living creature in the sea died. 4Then the third angel poured out his bowl on the rivers and springs of water, and they became blood.

5And I heard the angel of the waters saying: "You are righteous, O Lord, The One who is and who was and who is to be, Because You have judged these things. 6For they have shed the blood of saint sand prophets, And You have given them blood to drink. For it is their just due."

Hebrews 3:12-15 says;

Take care, brothers, lest there be in any of you an evil, unbelieving heart, leading you to fall away from the living God. But exhort one another every day, as long as it is called "today," that none of you may be hardened by the deceitfulness of sin.

For we have come to share in Christ, if indeed we hold our original confidence firm to the end. As it is said, "Today, if you hear his voice, do not harden your hearts as in the rebellion."

If we consider these messages, we could see that there is a tribunal that we need to face individually and account for our deeds as required by the Master.

This time there will be no lawyer who will advocate to for us. There will be no time to explain your words for the Judge. Everyone will even short words and will be wondering on how his or her life will be.

The Bible says; if you hear His voice, do not harden your heart as in the rebellion. Who will be your Lawyer at that moment? How will you see yourself in that day? Have you prepared for that day? How can you stand? Now let us consider our ways and doings and make the most for our life.

There is no time for evil deeds and waste. Be on your guard and wait vigilantly for the Master of His return. Who can stand before God? We have case to share with the Master; the Heavens and the Earth Creator; He is I am that I am coming with His reward to give to everyone according to his or her doings! You need to learn a lot and consider all your actions.

12. What is His Name?

Why Moses asked for the name of the Lord and what must we learn from it? What will be the benefit from that name and why is it important to know who sent Moses name?

In fact, Israelites forgot their fathers God due to their situation and long of the years they had in Egypt. The knowledge of God loss from their mind and forgot even the name of their fathers God. Their situation was terrible and disgrace.

Though some of them do remembered the promise of their deliverance told by Joseph and their fathers. But they forgot it through their hardship condition. Their condition was a burdensome and tough.

They all lost hope of deliverance and even faith to pursue God as their hope. Moses asked God name because even he himself has forgot the God of Abraham, Isaac and Jacob.

He did not even remember the God of his fathers until he was approach by God Himself. He hid his face on the ground and was afraid to look at God. In life, we always forget God our creator when things go well or even when it becomes hard sometimes, unless we approach by Him or through His message or words.

God always remember us and we are present before Him every day. He has engraved us in His palms and our walls are always before Him. We are not left alone; God is always near to help. It's sometimes seems that we are alone and abandon that we have been forgotten by God.

Here, Moses was afraid to look at God when he first time heard of Him. Years and hardship led Moses forgot God and even His name. Our cry have reach the God of sabaoth and He will deliver us in due time. He is concerned about our suffering and He is ready to rescue us from our fears.

Moses was sent by God to deliver Israel from their bondage and he was afraid to go. He question God on other matters and resisted not to go to where he has been sent.

We sometimes afraid to failed when we are turning into a new job or work. We do doubt about how it will be and what will come from it. Moses question God and demand security to fulfill his mission. He asks the name of Him who is sending him.

He demanded power and authority of God to awaking the faith of those who he has been sent to them. As human beings; we always want to see miracles of God before believing Him. But the Bibles says bless are those who didn't see and have believe. We need to have faith in God and trust His words.

Moses asked the name of the Lord to have a firm foundation to proof his mission. His word was what shall I say to them? Supposing them asked of your name? What is His name? God said to Moses, I AM WHO I AM. I am has sent me to you.

The name of the Lord is difficult to pronounce and understand. The real name of the Lord God is (**YHWH**) which is now pronouncing Yahweh (Jehovah).

No one can pronounce the name of the Lord God of Israel. This means that, He (God) is all in all and there is none like Him. All power belongs to Him. He is the Creator of the universe and the source of life.

His name is I am that I am. We are His creatures and glory. We need not to fear of want or discourage in hard times. Let's trust God and His words, and then all things will work together for our good. His name is our defender and shield.

The name of the Lord is strong towers the righteous who run unto it have a refuge. His name identifies His authority and character. He is our source of life and everything concerning life. His name is Immanuel means God is with us.

He is Alpha and Omega, the beginning and the end. He loves us and wishes our good. He loves us equal to Himself. He is ever ready to die and recue us from all dangers. All that we need to do is to trust Him and rely on Him. His name is I am who I am!

13. Trust God

We need no other witness or evidence to know who God is. All things whether above or on earth testifies His ability and love. He created the world out of nothing and called the host of them from nowhere.

Who have seen God and been His counselor before? We know no how He came into being and cannot explain His works and doings. He is eternal God and Jehovah is His name.

We need not to question Him or ask of His doings. We are His creatures and glory of His being. His words are sure and everlasting.

Many people do not understand the works and doing of the Lord. Others fail to trust Him and His words. His ways are not our ways and His thoughts and time are not ours. He has thousand ways to provide for us in which we know nothing.

Sometimes, we think that God's time is difficult to wait for and it is not favorable for our needs. We always want things fast and time that we wishes. But God wait to do our wishes not as time that we wish. So, many are dying without hope. We must trust God and wait for His time that will bring us abundant peace and wellbeing. We need not to fear and be discourage.

Who knows the best times for our success? Never take God less or distrusted His words. Who made the Heavens and the Earth? Who created you? Who knows the end from the beginning? Our life is not ours to make it better, why because we cannot do anything without Him.

Never doubt of God or be discourage when things move wrong. Circumstances are His workmanship for our progress. Moses was afraid to go to Egypt and wanted God to send someone else instead of him (Moses).

We sometimes forget what who God is and doubt about Him. God is always with us, ready to help. He will never fail or forsake us and ever willing to support and sustain us.

We need to have courage and enthusiasm that God will do above what we think or ask concerning ourselves. You do not to worry about tomorrow or your future how will it be. Leave everything to God and trust Him. It is not over at your age whether you are older or not.

Bless are they that wait upon the Lord, they will mount as eagle, they will walk or run and not be weary. You need to know who God is and what you can be through His help. He is our creator, He never leave us or forsake us as His creatures.

What we need to do is to trust and seek first His kingdom and all things will be added unto us. The higher than highest of life idea and the ideal of character that is resemblance to His character; that He (God) wants for us to possess. He wants our good and progress.

He can do all things and can damage all things and can repair all things. Do not fear for wants and never be discouraged about your life, leave everything to God and wait for His due time. He is ever ready to help, to rescue and redeem. Just trust Him and believe His words.

14. Here am I

We need to be ready for God's mission. The world is run out and people are dying with no hope. Are you ready to work for God or wish to do your own thing? Moses responses to God show his readiness.

Moses led his flock to wilderness and came to the mountain of God. He saw a burning bush and wanted to know why the bush was burning but not consumed? He heard the voice calling him out from the bush and he was afraid to hear the voice that calls him.

It is a voice of God; his father's God and hides his face because he was afraid to look at God of his fathers'. The beauty of this incident is that, Moses wasn't heard God's voice before and he became afraid to look at Him.

Have you ever heard God's voice before? How did you respond to it? Will be you afraid to hear God's voice for the first time? What will be your answer to Him? We are almost homes; the world is going to an end.

There are rumor of wars all over everywhere. People are fighting for liberty and refuge. Others do not know what to do. Many are dying and others have loss hope of life. There are noises everywhere calling for help.

Israelites were afraid and wanting to have liberty of their life. Do you remember when you became worried and wanted death to life? This world has so many lessons that need to be study and find out why is it so?

Our hopes sometimes dyed off and life becomes burdensome. In fact, there is thing hard than best life achievement. God needs you to go the world and comfort and rescue the perishing. Everywhere in the globe is darkened; hopes are gone and fear always approach in some of the people's life.

We need to prepare ourselves for soul winning. Many people are dying and some are been deceived by the devil. We have work to do, it is time to let people know the hour we are in and then rescue the perishing souls.

Moses responds to the message of God and went as the call came. We are to go as we have been told as did Moses. Let's read what Jesus said to His disciples;

Matthew 28:19-20

[19]Therefore go and make disciples of all nations, baptizing them in the name of the Father and of the Son and of the Holy Spirit, [20]and teaching them to obey everything I have commanded you. And surely I am with you always, to the very end of the age."

We must go and make disciples of all nations and to teach them to obey everything that God has commanded us. Moses went to Egypt and rescue the Israelites from bondage; so we are to go and rescue people's from their sins through the word of God.

It is everyone duty to do something for God that will result in the soul winning. Our talents and gifts are given to let people know who God is and it is our duty to use for the glory of God and to rescue the souls through it performance.

We have no excuse; it is our duty to let people know God through our gifts performance. The world is going to an end. Many people are crying for help and liberation from their sins.

Their burdens are weighing them down and their hope has loss. Others are weighing down by poverty and disease; we are to go and reach for them and comfort them by the word of God.

As Moses went to Egypt and deliver the Israelites; so we are to do same to our brothers and sisters who are in sin bondage. God is sending us to preach the gospel to the poor and rescue them from their burdens.

Do not be selfish but share what you have and make someone glorify God through your positive impact.

We have more to do and to share the Gospel message to others who are struggle with sin. Then save them from their burdens. We must say; here am I like Moses and Isaiah send me Lord. Who will go for us? Here am I.

15. Moses in Egypt

What will happen if we go as God has commanded us? Miracles will follow us when we go; many will be delivered from sins and bondage of life. Moses did many miracles in Egypt and at the end the Israelites were delivered.

In Egypt there were many incidences that delayed Moses in his work of deliverance of the Israelites. In fact, there are forces of powers everywhere in the globe. But all power has been given to Christ both Heaven and the Earth. He is the Captain and the leader of the race.

We need not to fear the willies of the enemy. Moses faced a lot of hesitations and rejection of Pharaoh but he prevails at the end. We shall face all the attacks of the enemy but it is attack of no results.

We have the leader who has been conquer the enemy before and there is nothing that can block us from winning the battle. The Egyptians tried it but they failed. If God is for us, who can be against us? Now, let's read some texts from the Bible and see what happen when Moses got to the seen.

Exodus 4:18-31

Read;

[18]Then Moses went back to Jethro his father-in-law and said to him, "Let me return to my own people in Egypt to see if any of them are still alive."

Jethro said, "Go, and I wish you well."

[19]Now the Lord had said to Moses in Midian, "Go back to Egypt, for all those who wanted to kill you are dead." [20]So Moses took his wife and sons, put them on a donkey and started back to Egypt. And he took the staff of God in his hand.

[21] The Lord said to Moses, "When you return to Egypt, see that you perform before Pharaoh all the wonders I have given you the power to do. But I will harden his heart so that he will not let the people go.

[22] Then say to Pharaoh, 'This is what the Lord says: Israel is my firstborn son, [23] and I told you, "Let my son go, so he may worship me." But you refused to let him go; so I will kill your firstborn son.'"

[24] At a lodging place on the way, the Lord met Moses and was about to kill him. [25] But Zipporah took a flint knife, cut off her son's foreskin and touched Moses' feet with it. "Surely you are a bridegroom of blood to me," she said. [26] So the Lord let him alone. (At that time she said "bridegroom of blood," referring to circumcision.)

[27] The Lord said to Aaron, "Go into the wilderness to meet Moses." So he met Moses at the mountain of God and kissed him. [28] Then Moses told Aaron everything the Lord had sent him to say, and also about all the signs he had commanded him to perform.

[29] Moses and Aaron brought together all the elders of the Israelites, [30] and Aaron told them everything the Lord had said to Moses. He also performed the signs before the people,

[31] and they believed. And when they heard that the Lord was concerned about them and had seen their misery, they bowed down and worshiped.

As Christians are God's children and it is our duty to deliver our brothers and sisters who the enemy has captured them into captivity. Though we shall face a lot of trials and tribulations but we need to do our part honestly for God is with us. We are not left alone, He is always with us. Miracles and wonders will follow us which the devil cannot withstand.

Let's consider these texts and see what came out when Moses got there.

Read; Exodus 5, 6:1-12

5 Afterward Moses and Aaron went to Pharaoh and said, "This is what the Lord, the God of Israel, says: 'Let my people go, so that they may hold a festival to me in the wilderness.'"

²Pharaoh said, "Who is the Lord, that I should obey him and let Israel go? I do not know the Lord and I will not let Israel go."

³Then they said, "The God of the Hebrews has met with us. Now let us take a three-day journey into the wilderness to offer sacrifices to the Lord our God, or he may strike us with plagues or with the sword."

⁴But the king of Egypt said, "Moses and Aaron, why are you taking the people away from their labor? Get back to your work!" ⁵Then Pharaoh said, "Look, the people of the land are now numerous, and you are stopping them from working."

⁶That same day Pharaoh gave this order to the slave drivers and overseers in charge of the people: ⁷"You are no longer to supply the people with straw for making bricks; let them go and gather their own straw.

⁸But require them to make the same number of bricks as before; don't reduce the quota. They are lazy; that is why they are crying out, 'Let us go and sacrifice to our God.' ⁹Make the work harder for the people so that they keep working and pay no attention to lies."

¹⁰Then the slave drivers and the overseers went out and said to the people, "This is what Pharaoh says: 'I will not give you any more

straw. ¹¹Go and get your own straw wherever you can find it, but your work will not be reduced at all.'"

¹²So the people scattered all over Egypt to gather stubble to use for straw. ¹³The slave drivers kept pressing them, saying, "Complete the work required of you for each day, just as when you had straw."

¹⁴And Pharaoh's slave drivers beat the Israelite overseers they had appointed, demanding, "Why haven't you met your quota of bricks yesterday or today, as before?"

¹⁵Then the Israelite overseers went and appealed to Pharaoh: "Why have you treated your servants this way? ¹⁶Your servants are given no straw, yet we are told, 'Make bricks!' Your servants are being beaten, but the fault is with your own people."

¹⁷Pharaoh said, "Lazy, that's what you are—lazy! That is why you keep saying, 'Let us go and sacrifice to the Lord.' ¹⁸Now get to work. You will not be given any straw, yet you must produce your full quota of bricks."

¹⁹The Israelite overseers realized they were in trouble when they were told, "You are not to reduce the number of bricks required of you for each day."

²⁰When they left Pharaoh, they found Moses and Aaron waiting to meet them, ²¹and they said, "May the Lord look on you and judge you! You have made us obnoxious to Pharaoh and his officials and have put a sword in their hand to kill us."

²²Moses returned to the Lord and said, "Why, Lord, why have you brought trouble on this people? Is this why you sent me? ²³Ever

since I went to Pharaoh to speak in your name, he has brought trouble on this people, and you have not rescued your people at all."

6 Then the Lord said to Moses, "Now you will see what I will do to Pharaoh: Because of my mighty hand he will let them go; because of my mighty hand he will drive them out of his country."

[2]God also said to Moses, "I am the Lord. [3]I appeared to Abraham, to Isaac and to Jacob as God Almighty, but by my name the Lord I did not make myself fully known to them.

[4]I also established my covenant with them to give them the land of Canaan, where they resided as foreigners. [5]Moreover, I have heard the groaning of the Israelites, whom the Egyptians are enslaving, and I have remembered my covenant.

[6]"Therefore, say to the Israelites: 'I am the Lord, and I will bring you out from under the yoke of the Egyptians. I will free you from being slaves to them, and I will redeem you with an outstretched arm and with mighty acts of judgment.

[7]I will take you as my own people, and I will be your God. Then you will know that I am the Lord your God, who brought you out from under the yoke of the Egyptians.

[8]And I will bring you to the land I swore with uplifted hand to give to Abraham, to Isaac and to Jacob. I will give it to you as a possession. I am the Lord.'"

[9]Moses reported this to the Israelites, but they did not listen to him because of their discouragement and harsh labor.

[10]Then the Lord said to Moses, [11]"Go, tell Pharaoh king of Egypt to let the Israelites go out of his country."

[12]But Moses said to the Lord, "If the Israelites will not listen to me, why would Pharaoh listen to me, since I speak with faltering lips

In fact, we will face a lot of hardships and discouragement when we go and preach the gospel. There will be a struggle in the deliverance of the people who the devil has captured them. But he has been already conquered by Christ.

We need not feel disappointed as did Moses when he first faced trouble and rejection. But we must do move as He (God) commanded us, and there will be a victory at the end. Unless we fail the Master concerning our own acts and doings.

Moses did many wonders in Egypt when he got there. Wonders shall follow us after the work is done. Our duty is to go as He has commanded us. There will be a lot of fight but souls must be delivering from their sins. We must do the work according to what He (God) commanded us.

There will be a massive and good result. We should not be discouraged when things happen in the manner that we don't expect. Life has become struggle because of sin. The enemy life has cross obstacles in everywhere in the globe fighting to destroy souls for eternal doom.

But we must go as the Master has commanded us to go to Egypt and rescue His people who the devil has captured and deliver them. Are you on your way going or doing your own thing?

For good life living and salvation reward
BBS LIFE BOOKS
The Strange Voice Page

Did you love *The Strange Voice*? Then you should read *A shelter from storm and rain*[1] by Bernard Benson Sarfo!

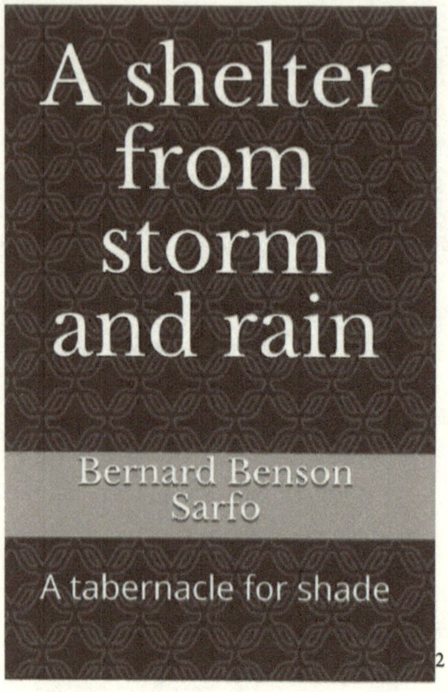

[2]

Is there anyone who can help you than Christ? Who is a life giver and who created life? Who has risen from the death before? Is there any life beyond life? Yes; it is.

What do you want to know? What do you want to see? There is no peace on this earth and no one who can solve problems of a man. A shelter from storm and rain is as this book title refers to Christ. He is our only shade from the heat of a sun or the defense of all our problems.

---

1. https://books2read.com/u/3RwPDL

2. https://books2read.com/u/3RwPDL

He is the one who can help you totally without any inconveniences. He is the one who the world need most. He is the word of God who the world was created through Him.

He is the light of the world and the redeemer of mankind. You need no other one but Christ. He is the one who everyone is looking for Him. He holds something uniquely and comfortable for man.

In Him was life and the life was the light of man. You need no other witness that Jesus die for you. He is alive to help and rescue those who will call for Him. He is the one among thousands and the king among kings. He is the way; the truth and the life. There are cries everywhere on the globe. People do not have peace; our ways are dark and evil every day. We are all dying and wailing; our hopes have gone and there is no help. Now is the time for you to seek God and live.

The whole world is in crisis and there is nothing that can helps or comforts us. It is time to seek God and live. He is the only solution to our problems. We need no other one; except Christ Jesus who dies on the cross for the entire world.

He is the one who can help and rescue us from this calamity which is in the world today. He is the one who the world need now and most. What have you considered?

Also by Bernard Benson Sarfo

The Fact Among Facts (1st)
The Fact Among Facts

Standalone
The Youth Murderer
Be Original Not a Copy
The Christians Science or Scholarship
Precious than Paradise
Habit makes future
A shelter from storm and rain
The Science of Life
The Strongest Lion Knockback
The Perfect and Inspiring City
Above Hope, Faith and Love
The Hero's Brave Decisions
The Weakest Among Plants
The Hero's Brave Decisions
Doing Above The Ability
The Wisdom Beyond Power And Greatness

Heavier Than the Heavens
The Academics Brains and Recreation Logics
The Strange Voice

About the Author

Bernard Benson Sarfo is an acquainted architectural designer and a motivational speaker.He is a gifted teacher who continues to motivate and encourage many.

Read more at https://www.amazon.com//author/bbslifebooks.

www.ingramcontent.com/pod-product-compliance
Lightning Source LLC
Chambersburg PA
CBHW020119180726
47992CB00019B/1029